Creating a Good Self-Image in Your Child

Bill E. Forisha, Ph.D.,
and Penelope B. Grenoble, Ph.D.

CB

CONTEMPORARY
BOOKS

CHICAGO · NEW YORK

Published by Contemporary Books, Inc.
180 North Michigan Avenue, Chicago, Illinois 60601
Manufactured in the United States of America
International Standard Book Number: 0-8092-4672-4

Published simultaneously in Canada by Beaverbooks, Ltd.
195 Allstate Parkway, Valleywood Business Park
Markham, Ontario L3R 4T8 Canada

ACKNOWLEDGMENTS

Special thanks to Keshav Kamath, who worked on the preparation of this manuscript, and to Creighton Grenoble for computer assistance.

—PBG

Thanks also to Mary Ann Bockbrader for "active listening" at a moment of intense frustration.

—BEF

CONTENTS

An Introduction to *ParentBooks That Work*

I t has been said that twenty-five-dollar words can be used to cover up twenty-five-cent ideas. In our increasingly technological society, jargon and complex language often confuse the meaning of information. This is particularly the case in the social and psychological sciences.

The "hard sciences" such as physics, chemistry, and biology have an advantage: there is little chance, for example, that a photon or a quark will be confused with something else.

In the human sciences, however, we have at least two problems with language. One is that the popular definition of a word such as *sex* or *intelligence* can differ considerably from the way a professional in the field might use it. Although we parents share a common pool of language with social scientists and teachers and therapists, words like *input* and *reinforcement*, *expectations* and *assessment*, mean one thing to parents and another to social science experts. Thus the danger that we will not understand each other is very real.

The human sciences' other language problem is jargon. A particular group of human scientists may develop obscure or seemingly incomprehensible language as a shortcut to communication among its members. Thus, jargon can be a roadblock when the experts try to talk to people outside their field.

The books in this series are the result of skillful collaboration between trained psychologists experienced in family and child development and a seasoned writer. The authors have strived to take twenty-five-dollar ideas and deliver them in language that is clear, concise, and most useful to you. In these six books, the emphasis is on presenting intelligent and practical ideas that you can use to help solve the age-old problems of child rearing.

This brings us to the very reason for these books. It might have occurred to you to ask, "Why should I rely on so-called experts when I can fall back on tradition and conventional wisdom? After all, the human race has survived well on what parents have taught children through the ages." Think about that for a moment. In the long history of human life on this planet, most of our energy has been spent in survival against the elements. It's only in most recent history that we've enjoyed the luxury to live, rather than simply survive. The fact is that the help and advice children need most nowadays has to do with a different level of survival in a world we've created ourselves, a complex world of rapid change.

Even though at moments nature can remind us of her often terrible wrath and power, most of our problems are still manmade. What we—parents and children both—have to learn is to deal with a reality that we have created ourselves.

In the bewildering array of cultures, creeds, and cross-purposes that are modern life, we need a special set of skills to live and be productive. Competition is an essential fact of life. Your child faces stress and pressure from society's expectations from the day he or she is born. To get through, your child needs the best help you can give.

The position of the professional expert is new and revered in our society. The expert is one of our cleverest inventions. Involved in the intense study of one problem or subject, the expert comes to know it better than anyone else. We trust the expert because we know that we don't have the time or ability to sort out everything ourselves. And, if the expert follows the best instincts of his profession, his high level of professional competence will serve you. By using the specialized knowledge of the expert, parents can face the difficult but practical problems of building a family and preparing their children to meet the demands of early childhood and elementary school.

Enlightened by this advice, we can give our children a healthy attitude and a better chance.

These concise and practical books deal with some of the most important issues in young children's lives today. They will help you to help your child and to feel good about your role as a parent. With this in mind, we dedicate this series to you.

Richard H. Thiel, Ph.D.
California State University

INTRODUCTION

Feeling good about yourself, and about the image other people have of you, is important to every one of us. The problem is that we sometimes like to believe that we can accomplish this by the sheer effort of positive thinking. We hope that if we're optimistic we can conquer all our doubts and fears. Although it would be wonderful if that were the case, we can't *will* away years of bad experiences that may cause us to feel bad about who we are and what we project to others. The key is to *prevent* our bad habits from getting us into trouble in the first place.

We all know children who seem to be constantly down, who don't feel good about themselves, who are afraid to try. Such children fear that there is something wrong with them, that somehow they don't measure up. Often these children see the world as a very hostile place. They experience little joy.

They have little chance of developing a positive self-image and thinking well of themselves.

Feeling good about yourself is based on the belief that you have talents and abilities that you have taken advantage of. Additionally, you can't think positively about yourself unless you value who you are. And strange as it may seem, for all of us this process begins in infancy. Thus, our goal is to show that you can help your child grow up to feel good about himself, what the experts call having a good sense of self-esteem. No amount of positive thinking ("Every day, in every way, I'm getting better") can help a child who has failed to discover and use his potential. Your child must constantly be allowed to test his capabilities and learn from his successes and errors. Through this experimentation he will build the sturdy foundation of self-esteem necessary for adult life.

This sense of self-esteem or worth grows as your child adjusts to the things around him. If your child encounters warmth and nurturing, if he gets his needs met, and if his caretakers are involved with him, then he will begin to feel that the world is okay. The experts refer to this as the child's feeling that he is lovable and worthwhile.

Feeling worthwhile is based on feelings of being able to do things well and of being important to other people. These feelings have their origin in the first year of life. For example, a mother who is distracted or uninterested when she is bathing or diapering her child will communicate a sense of indifference. The infant will not *know* what this means, but he does recognize feelings of warmth and attention and involvement or their absence. Infants are constantly evaluating their experiences based on whether they are pleasurable or painful. A child's experiences as an infant will lay the foundation for his expectations for the rest of his life. A child who is neglected for some reason or is deprived of attention from his parents, expecially early, will begin to fear that there is something wrong with him. If this continues, he may doubt himself, fear that he can't do anything right, and finally give up.

In this book, which is designed to help you help your child develop a healthy image of himself, we'll first look at the things your child may face growing up in today's society. Then we'll look at what he should be accomplishing at various ages and stages of childhood. After that, we'll offer some guidelines for you to observe whether or not your child is achieving the tasks required of his age. Finally we'll present practical suggestions for helping your child grow up healthy and feeling good about himself.

As in all books in this series, references typically refer to children with male pronouns such as he or his; please keep in mind that we are thinking of your daughter also. In today's competitive world, it is very important that she thinks well of herself and has a high sense of self-esteem.

Part I
Understanding
The Concept of
Self-Esteem

For both you and your child, that wonderful sense of feeling good about yourself, commonly known as self-esteem, is based on the feeling that you are productive and that your contributions are valued. Also important to your sense of self-esteem is how you yourself value your accomplishments.

For your child the process begins by facing the challenges of his life as he grows from infancy to preadolescence and beyond. Educators and psychologists call these challenges *developmental tasks*. In childhood they correspond (although sometimes imperfectly) to your child's chronological age. Each involves a turning point of childhood, sometimes called a psychological-social crisis. These big words only mean that to grow and develop, your child must face and overcome a series of predictable experiences.

It is your job to help your child confront and complete each of these successfully, because each is the foundation for the next stage. Failure inhibits your child's ability to progress and may cause severe difficulties later in life. You should view these "crises" as essential to growth, and you should not attempt to shield your child from what may seem like traumatic experiences. A child who avoids confronting the demands of growing up, especially early in life, is in danger of withdrawing from all challenges. The resulting decrease in self-respect will cause him to fail in the future and severely damage his sense of self-esteem.

A child with low self-esteem will view himself as having little worth; he will feel he has nothing particular to offer to society and will expect to be exploited and taken advantage of. He will be guarded and defensive in his interactions with other family members. Additionally, he will develop indifference or hostility toward himself and other people. Surely you do not want that for your child. And it needn't happen. A few guiding principles will help you understand the challenges your child will face and how you may best aid him on his way to maturity.

SELF-ESTEEM AND ITS RELATIONSHIP TO THE FAMILY

Children usually grow and develop in a family environment. In essence, they are a product of the family. In today's world, however, most of the traditional social supports for the family—such as the church, the extended family, having one parent consistently

at home, long-term marriages—have been significantly reduced. Given the pressures that beset parents and children alike, it is often very difficult to
sense whether your family is developing in a healthy
way or is on a collision course with crisis. You should
keep the following things in mind, however.

Communication

Communication is an essential element in the estab-
lishment of a solid, happy family, and it is one of the
first factors you should think about when evaluating
your family's ability to enhance your child's self-
esteem. Dr. Virginia Satir, a family therapist and one
of the world's foremost experts on family interaction, has pioneered work on the family communication process.

Members of a family that is nurturing and productive communicate directly and clearly with each
other. They are honest with each other and trust
each other. Most of all, they are not afraid to talk
about their feelings with each other.

In such families, which help children gain high
self-esteem, parents and child use what are referred
to as "I" statements. They will say, "I think" or "I
feel" instead of the impersonal, "It seems like."
These families also put limits on a child's behavior.
Rules are flexible and are subject to change, both as
the child grows and as the family changes. What you
would expect of a child of three is different from one
of six, and so will be the guidelines you establish for
his behavior.

Most of all, in families where communication is

good, parents and child feel happy being members of the family. The child contributes to the family's well-being and, even as late as adolescence, will find time to spend with the family. Home will always be a secure place for him, and he will feel good retreating to it. People in such families will feel that they are living with people whom they can trust and who trust them on a very basic level.

Finally, both parents and children will also have the communication skills to have open and flexible relationships with other people outside the family—teachers, friends, and neighbors. A child in a family where there is little communication will be depressed and hostile. (It's important to note that we are speaking not of simple anger, but of patterns of persistent hostility toward oneself or others, which indicate that the child is not feeling good about himself. A persistent pattern of this kind over a long time is what parents should be alert to.) His hostility comes from the realization that family members are trying to manipulate him and each other to achieve what they want. The result is that family members are constantly defensive. Because they are constantly challenged rather than nurtured, their self-esteem is always at stake and fragile. Communication is indirect and there is a constant need to read between the lines—because that is where the real clues are.

Rules

Troubled families either set rigid rules for a child's behavior, or the rules are so flexible that the child has no sense of his limits. Rigid rules are dangerous because they are usually arbitrary, and authoritarian measures of discipline are often used to enforce the rules. In overly permissive families, on the other hand, there is a constant process of negotiation between parents and children. Problems are seldom really resolved and the children suffer from feeling isolated and without guidance.

Because your child experiences his first relationships within your family, it's important that you are supportive, set rules and boundaries, and enforce them. You should also be honest and genuine in your responses to your child and other family members. You should never lie or exaggerate the truth. You should be responsible and dependable. It's important to be understanding and to listen empathetically to problems that other family members express, especially if they relate to family rules and your expectations for your children. And you should give your child a definite sense that the world is a good place to be. You should look for the positive in other people and respect other people for who they are and what they do. You should show that you can make your own decisions about your life and that you have good relationships with your friends and other parents. Also you should let your child see that we all make mistakes at times. No one is perfect and trying to be can be frustrating and threatening to self-esteem.

Society

In our ever-changing and complicated world, you need all the help you can get in being a positive model for your child and helping him to grow up. Traditionally, parents were aided by members of the extended family, who could step in and help, especially if both parents needed to be outside of the home a great deal. Over the years, social changes have interfered with this process. Mobility has decreased relationships with members of the extended family, and parents have had to rely on various types of outside help. Single parents and dual-career marriages have also reduced the amount of help and encouragement parents can give their children.

While it used to take several generations for changes in attitudes to take place, they can now occur within one generation. In the absence of help and support from grandparents, aunts, and uncles, parents often face answers to difficult questions in isolation. Do you encourage your three-year-old son to cry, for example, or do you do what parents have done for generations—suggest that it is not appropriate for boys to show emotion? Do you encourage your daughter to continue to be a tomboy even though she is at an age where she is "supposed" to be "acting like a girl"?

It is also a fact of life that we are influenced by television and other media. Where family input has decreased, television has stepped into the void. TV continues to be an intrusion in our lives, suggesting bad models and raising false expectations and hopes. Unfortunately, it is also used as a baby-sitter and a pacifier by many overworked parents. In families where communication is poor, TV deflects attention from family problems—and actually contributes to the lack of communication.

In today's society the best thing you can do is help your child be prepared to respond to change, which is our way of life. He can do this, however, only if he has a good sense of himself. The child who feels good about himself will be confident to meet life's demands, but a child with little self-esteem will flounder and fail, especially when faced with a number of confusing demands. Afraid to try, he will never succeed.

If you are aware of the influence on your family, you can counteract the effects of television and other media, and you can maximize the benefits of outside help that you may need to care for your child— whether it be the baby-sitter or the teacher in preschool.

The process of childhood is an exciting and challenging experience for you and your child, a time of discovering the world for your child, and an opportunity to share his joy and delight. Our suggestions for helping your child develop will only work in a happy family, where communication is open and honest.

You will need to pay attention to your child. You will need to be affectionate *and* you will have to make rules and enforce them. One of your primary jobs is to listen to your child and respond. The other is to be an example of the behavior you expect of him. Read on, and we'll show you how.

Part II
Understanding
Your Child's
Development

There are five primary stages of growth children go through on their way to becoming adults. The first two stages are infancy and early childhood; stage three refers to middle childhood, the early school years; stage four covers the middle school years; and stage five is adolescence, the early teen years. During all five periods your child will be evaluating himself, forming his identity, and it's important that he complete each stage successfully. Let's look more closely at the various periods of childhood and the challenges that your child must complete.

STAGE ONE: INFANCY
(BIRTH TO AGE TWO)

The first of your child's developmental stages begins at birth and continues until approximately age two. The essential task an infant faces is learning to trust the people in his world. If he develops trust at this stage, he will learn to have faith not only in others, but in himself as well.

During the initial years of development, your child is at one with whoever is the primary caretaker, generally a parent. For all intents and purposes, the infant has no real sense that he's a separate person.

It is essential that your infant is attached to one person; usually this will be his mother. He will want to have his needs met by someone close and also be able to make his needs known to that person. He will need to learn that his smile makes you happy and that what he requires to survive (at this stage, food, sleep, warmth, and well-being) will be made available in response to his own actions.

On the other hand, if this close relationship does not happen, your child may be apprehensive and scared. He may feel that he will not be cared for, that no matter what he does—smiles, cries, giggles, or screams—he will not succeed in having his needs met. If a parent or caretaker considers childcare more a chore than a joy, your child will sense it. Often this is not intentional. A working mother may be distracted by problems of the office, a nanny by difficulties in her own life, a day-care worker by the demands of having too many children to take care of. Regardless, a child in such a situation is getting off to a bad start. You should pay careful attention to the arrangements you make for childcare, especially at this age.

An infant who lacks love and attention will show it. It's normal, for example, for an infant to turn to his mother if there's a stranger present. Likewise, a baby often cries when his mother goes out of sight. However, if your child still shows such behavior during the second year of life, especially with relatives or friends the child has often seen, you should be concerned. Turning his head away, drawing back his hand from people he knows are signs of unhappiness, especially if he seems to cry a lot for no reason and doesn't laugh much.

The most important thing you can provide at this stage is someone who can respond to your infant's needs. If you can't do this, you should make arrangements to see that your child has consistent care, complete with smiles and cuddling. This encourages a slow, safe separation into toddlerhood.

STAGE TWO: TODDLERHOOD (AGES TWO TO FOUR)

Toddlerhood involves a great deal of physical exploration, with a lot of enjoyable fantasy and play. Your child will also start to talk during this time.

Toddlers continue to explore things much as they did as infants. Learning is physical (such as when a baby grabs things and puts them in his mouth). Given their expanded strength and mobility, toddlers will move things from one place to another, explore their house or apartment, and discover the world around them.

If in infancy your child learned that he can have an impact on his world, and he feels good about that as a toddler, he will begin to be more independent. The important thing for you to remember is that he needs to feel that what he does is okay. He needs to trust you, and eventually himself, and to be independent. Trust will help him in future relationships, and independence will make him be productive.

Your toddler will want to be able to take care of himself. This is important; if he stays dependent on his mother or other caretakers, he'll never grow up. A happy toddler will laugh and do things spontaneously. He'll want to discover things on his own and may not want you to help him. Parents generally refer to this stage as the terrible twos. Although it may be frustrating to you, it's important for your child to be able to say no. It is part of the necessary dissociation from parents, and you should actually take delight in the fact that your child is forming an active personality.

If you don't let your child explore and try things, he may feel guilty. He may also think he's *not able* to do new things. What happens then is that he may fall back into things he already knows how to do. He may be impulsive and do things over and over again.

Jamie, for example, was a child who was very shy and depressed. He didn't eat well and his parents said he wasn't interested in new toys, but just sat and played in one corner of the bedroom. Jamie's mother and father were divorced, and he was often cared for by his grandmother, who was rather stern and was angry at Jamie's father for deserting the family. Jamie had learned that when his grandmother was around, certain kinds of behavior were okay and others were not. He was afraid to try new things and to make up new games, because he didn't want to anger his grandmother. Although she believed she was helping by setting limits, Jamie's grandmother was not letting him grow up.

Eventually, when the whole family went for therapy, Jamie's grandmother admitted her anger that the family had been broken up. The therapist taught her how to suggest new activities and to encourage her grandson to explore new games and play. Slowly Jamie became interested in his toys and in playing with other children.

Other toddlers, such as *Samantha*, are punished because they don't act like their parents want them to. Samantha's mother works all day as an executive secretary and doesn't like to see the house a mess when she comes home. She has insisted that Samantha learn to put her toys in their proper place. For Samantha this means putting each toy into her toy chest as soon as she has finished playing with it. She even takes toys away from her playmates—even if they are still using them—to put them back into the chest or in their place in her room. Also, Samantha likes to color, and her parents bought her a number of coloring books. Although she has colored most of them more than once, she always asks her parents to buy the same books over and over again, so that she can practice choosing the right colors and getting the shapes colored in correctly. Samantha would really like to have a new book, but she's afraid that she won't be able to color it right.

Children are transparent, and a child who is doing the same thing over and over will have a frown on his face. *Repetitive behavior is often an indication that your child is not becoming independent of your control and isn't developing.*

Often parents are too rigid in directing their children's play, establishing goals and timetables for completion. Your toddler will sense what kind of play and exploring is okay for him. You are wiser, however, and must be prepared to set limits, especially so your toddler won't be a nuisance to the rest of the family. Your best bet is to be flexible. In a case like Samantha's, for example, you might try having one room in the house—perhaps the child's own— where toys can be left out from time to time.

Besides physical exploration, your child's developing speech may produce some unpleasant results occasionally. Three- and four-year-olds, for example, love to experiment with "bad" words. *Eddy* is the son of a career couple: his mother is a lawyer, and his father a corporate executive who is also an attorney. Both parents have high expectations for their children. Their first son was doing well and so was their second son, Eddy, until a daughter was born. The new arrival demanded a lot of the parents' attention and the two boys didn't receive the care they were used to. Eddy was expelled from his private preschool because of bad language. He liked to use words like *shit* and *doo-doo* and make up rhymes such as "Lickety-split, doo-doo is shit."

His parents were frantic and sought counseling. First Eddy was referred for a complete physical and psychological workup, which indicated that he was healthy. The problem was that he was stuck and couldn't grow because he needed his parents' attention. Actually, it was his parents who needed therapy.

Eddy's parents were taught how to play so they could use play to interact with Eddy. They learned patty-cake and to say nonsense similar to what he had been spewing—doo-dah, doo-doo. They were embarrassed at first because they had been forbidden to use these words in their own families. Eventually they were able to play with Eddy and their other children. This helped them to show Eddy that he couldn't manipulate them with his bad behavior and that his parents did care for him. Within a week Eddy had given up his bad language.

Not long after, however, Eddy began to be depressed. Encouraged by their counselor, Eddie's parents hired a nanny to help with the new infant, and they both decided to spend more time with their family. Eddy's father began to take him along when he had errands to run on the weekends and even on short business trips. This showed Eddy that his father loved him and wanted to spend time with him. Gradually Eddy got better. His parents decided to keep the nanny, which actually gave them more time to spend with their children. They learned to enjoy some of the games they had been taught in therapy and within six weeks, Eddy was smiling again, happy and feeling that he had a place in the family.

A final word about toddlers. They often insist (sometimes quite strongly) that they be allowed to do things for themselves. This is not a whim, but an important part of growing up. Since toddlers learn by imitating others, they will spontaneously want to try everything they see others do. Though a parent's patience has limits, we advise you to extend yourself and tolerate your toddlers's inclination to experiment. A child too often prevented from doing things for himself—from tying his own shoe to playing a video game—will soon lose interest and want you to take care of him. You help best by offering gentle encouragement, and only coming to the child's rescue when he asks.

Take the case of Jimmy, for example. When Jimmy

and his father go to the supermarket together, Jimmy insists on taking each of the desired items off the shelf himself and putting it in the cart. Shopping trips with Jimmy take longer, but his father knows he will have to be patient. The same thing happens when they get the groceries home: Jimmy wants to help put the things away and protests loudly, throwing a minor tantrum, when someone else does it. During such outbursts, Jimmy's father joins in and shows—as Jamie's parents did—that such outbursts are not a threat, that they are rather silly and actually more fun than upsetting. Once during an outburst, Jimmy's father joined the noise-making by banging on some pots and pans. Soon he and his son were both on the floor laughing. After a hug, they put the groceries away together.

If you can provide a safe environment for your toddler to investigate and if you can tolerate his sometimes demanding behavior, you will be helping him grow with a good sense of self-esteem.

STAGE THREE: EARLY SCHOOL YEARS (AGES FOUR TO SIX)

The early school years, though not outwardly very different from toddlerhood, is a time of intense conceptual or more *intellectual* exploration, as opposed to the more *physical* exploration of toddlerhood. Children in the early school years seem to have unbounded curiosity about everything and will ask questions ranging from "Where do babies come from?" to "What happens after I die?"

Though toddlers usually begin to associate things

in the physical world with mental pictures and symbols, they can only communicate by action. Children in the early school years begin to be able to describe their actions verbally and may even begin performing such simple mental tasks as doing basic math or counting in their heads, rather than on their fingers.

Additionally, in toddlerhood your child was faced with wanting to be independent and with doubts about his exploring and experimenting. During the early school years, he *must* take initiative for action even if he feels a bit insecure about it. In order to be able to take initiative, your child will use the independence he fought for in toddlerhood. And so just as trust in infancy leads to an independent toddlerhood, so does toddlerhood independence lead to initiative in the early school years.

"Initiative" means both the active curiosity children normally have at this age and your child's growing sense of identity. Your child will need to learn to understand that he is a person who can do things, and what he does will become part of him—his personality. A two- or three-year-old may say no just to see what it feels like to say it. He may not really mean it but may need to explore the feeling. A four- to six-year-old, however, will say no for a reason. The initiative you see in your child will help him develop his ability to do things *for a purpose*, rather than the toddler's random exploring and experimenting.

Psychologists refer to this as *identification*, which means that the child has begun to identify himself with his own actions. Your child no longer randomly copies behavior; he now really wants to do things for himself. A three-year-old, for instance, may see

Mommy stacking dishes and will imitate the actions with play dishes while playing tea party. The four- to six-year-old, however will have "internalized" the dish stacking and wants to help put the real dishes away.

Nevertheless, children of this age will usually still identify particular behavior with the role models they initially imitated. In the example of dish stacking, the child will *believe* that certain dishes go only where his parents put them. This identification with parents is also exemplified when, say, a five-year-old insists that a baby-sitter use the same pan Mommy does to make an omelette, or that a story should be read or told in the particular way that Daddy uses. At this age, the child believes that the only way to do something is the way his parents do it, because that is what he has had the most experience with. To the child, this is the only right way to do things. Your behavior and the expectations for that behavior have become internalized; they are now part of your child's identity, but are still associated with you. Consequently, a child in the early school years still strongly identifies his self-image with you and your behavior. This is an important time for teaching by action, and you should be especially aware of what you do and how.

Your child will feel good about himself if his independently initiated actions are accomplished of his own free will. If, however, he has acted to avoid conflict, pain, or punishment, your child will feel guilty about his behavior. Thus, it is important that you're clear about your expectations for him during this time.

During ages two to four, a child easily picks up your spoken and implied message that you have expectations for him. Even toddlers realize that some things are OK to do and some are not. They learn this from limits imposed on them during their exploring. By the early school years, these messages have become part of your child's personality, and he replays them to himself, even if you no longer seem to actively insist on those limits. Of course, your child will respond to new expectations and limits from school and outside the home, which he will add to those he already understands and tries to live with.

If your child has not had opportunities for exploratory play in a safe environment as a toddler, he will not show initiative and spontaneity in the early school years. He may tend to give up and withdraw from continued exploration. He will feel guilty about what he does attempt, because he distrusts his ability. For a child of this age, guilt is expressed by too much concern with the shoulds and should nots. He will feel scared and hesitant; he will not trust himself to do anything right. He may feel guilty because he *should* have done something new or because he believes he can't live up to somebody's expectations of how something *should* be done.

Even if your child does meet the expectations of others, he may still feel guilty because he hasn't met his own internal expectations, which are sometimes vague and incomplete. He will be distrustful of his own responses to the world—of what he thinks and feels—and uncertain about other people's responses to him and his actions. This is most likely to happen when a child hasn't had enough time to experiment and try out new behaviors and know what doing new things feels like. Consequently, he will exhibit a kind of self-imposed restraint, which will become part of his personality.

If Jamie's situation with his grandmother had not been resolved as a toddler, he might have accepted the limits his grandmother had placed on him and been withdrawn and depressed in his early school years. Something of this kind was happening with *Alec*, a five-year-old who apparently was still caught in the problems of toddlerhood. When he started kindergarten, the teacher noticed that Alec always seemed anxious, especially when the class was beginning something new. Most of the other children were bouncing about and beside themselves with excitement. Alec pouted and sighed and refused to start anything on his own or to play games with the other children.

The teacher called Alec's mother, an outgoing, lively woman in her early thirties. She was shocked to find out how Alec was behaving. She agreed immediately to a conference with a special school team, including a psychologist. Her husband also came to the meeting and was equally surprised. A routine physical exam proved Alec healthy, and a preliminary rudimentary IQ test showed that he tested slightly above average. This didn't surprise Alec's parents, who had been drilling him in arithmetic and had even begun to teach him to read. They were very proud of their son.

The initiative taken by Alec's parents caused some concern among the school team. The parents were questioned about the kind of games and play Alec preferred. They mentioned some of the gifts they had bought for him: a microscope, chemistry set, a home computer. They said the microscope had interested him for a while; his father had shown him how to use it, and they had looked at slides together. But the boy "just didn't go anywhere in that direction." His father complained that Alec only seemed interested in looking at things and was not organized in what he did.

Asked if Alec drew or colored or made artsy-craftsy things, or whether he played with other children, his parents' responses began to make sense to Alec's teacher and the psychologist. His parents maintained that by their standards Alec was not a very good artist, though they had tried to encourage him in those directions. They complained his pictures didn't look like the things he was supposed to be drawing and seemed to have no artistic quality whatsoever. "We gave up on his being an artist at about the age of four," his mother said smiling.

As for playing with other children, Alec's first social contact was kindergarten. An only child, he had spent his time until that year in the home with his parents. His mother gave up her job when the boy was born and had considered going back to work only when he started school. She had devoted her time to providing interesting activities and playing games with him. It was obvious even during that informal meeting that on the one hand, Alec's parents had great expectations for their son, while on the other, they stifled his impulses by being dissatisfied with what he did attempt. Essentially Alec's parents had tried to ignore toddlerhood. In subsequent sessions, a frequent baby-sitter explained that Alec became extremely upset and moody when she did anything in a way that was different from what his parents did. His mother apparently had an odd habit when she gave the boy ice cream of alternating scoops for him and giving herself a scoop and licking the scooper. The baby-sitter did not do it that way, and Alec would angrily refuse to eat the ice cream. It was obvious that Alec was identifying too strongly with his parents and their expectations. He felt almost like he was "not there," that he wasn't an independent person.

Alec's parents began to be more flexible about allowing Alec to draw and engage in other creative play. Although it took time, Alec eventually enjoyed painting dogs that did not look like dogs. What his parents learned was that though their son would probably not be a Picasso, he needed to do things suitable for his age. They had not been aware that some things are beyond small children's capabilities.

Alec's art may never be exhibited in a museum, but it allowed him to display and enjoy his developing personality. It was important for his parents to encourage his efforts so that he could begin to feel good about himself.

It is at this stage of your child's life, for example, that you may walk into the living room and find that all the chairs and couches have been moved together with sheets and blankets spread over the top of them. Your child has created a cave out of the living room. Although your first reaction might be irritation that your living room furniture has been rearranged, you actually should be happy because your child is being imaginative and is taking initiative. Likewise, if you find that your best sheets have been sewn together and holes cut in them for Halloween costumes, you might try to hide your anger, praise his efforts, and explain that the next time he should ask for old sheets.

When your child does not greet the challenge of creativity with excitement but with fear and withdrawal, then you know he is not accomplishing the challenge of this age. If your efforts to help aren't successful, you should consider seeking therapeutic help from a family counselor.

The early school years are also the period when children form associations with the opposite-sex parent. Little boys begin to be more attached to their mothers, little girls to their fathers. This serves two purposes: It continues to enforce the growth of your child's personality as a separate person and helps him understand and define himself sexually. A boy will feel better about his gender if a mother acknowledges his plays for her attention. The same is true of girls and their fathers.

Sometimes this process can be difficult for the other parent, who may previously have been close to the child—especially if your child spontaneously seems to reject you in favor of your spouse. For instance, *Betty*, who had always wanted her mother to read stories to her and be the one she asked for things, suddenly decided she would rather that Daddy read a story or take a look at her drawing. *Jack*, who usually wanted his Dad to help him get ready for bed and tuck him in, suddenly decided he wanted his mother to watch him brush his teeth and kiss him good night. These children are broadening their range, so to speak, in seeking approval from the other parent. The attachment may even take on romantic overtones. Jack might say he wants to grow up and marry Mom; Betty may think that she wants to fall in love with her father. When this happens, you should not overreact. If you accept these shifts of affection and handle them gently and casually, your child will better be able to deal with sexuality and romance later in adolescence.

If you feel uneasy about all of this, you might feel better if you take a moment and think of your own childhood. For instance, if Betty's mother resents Betty's new attachment to her father, it may be that something is wrong with her own relationship with her husband. When she thought about it, Betty's mother did remember that when she was a little girl about her daughter's age, her father had not been around. Her parents had divorced, and she had not seen her father again until she was almost grown. So she became particularly upset when Betty began to reach out to her father and he responded. Betty's mom decided to seek help, and in therapy she discovered she was actually jealous of her little girl's relationship with Daddy. Her jealousy got in the way of her initial feelings of being loving and encouraging to her daughter.

During this age, boys and girls become very aware of their biological sex, an essential part of the emerging personality or self. They begin to understand that they are different from each other, partly by understanding the differences in behavior and outlook of their parents. Simultaneously, boys or girls also compare themselves with the same-sex parent to see how they're similar. The attachment to the opposite parent becomes important because it reflects how your child feels about the differences he sees. If you accept this, and the parent who feels like he or she is being rejected takes this in stride, your child will feel good about his sexuality. This process of sexual identification and differentiation begins to diminish after about age five or six.

During early school years, your child may become extremely self-centered. At this stage, children are struggling to emerge and feel good about the past six years—the whole of their experience. You might think of an image of your child "strutting his stuff." To other people it may seem like selfishness, or too much interest in himself, but it's necessary. High self-esteem is reflected in the enjoyment of the self and others, and if you respond with acceptance and joy that your child is meeting his challenges in growth and development, he'll be able to build from one stage to another. These early school years is usually the time when your child will question your godlike status as his parent so he can begin to develop faith in his own ability to become independent and fend for himself.

Common mistakes parents make during this time fall into two categories. Unprepared for all of this, parents attempt to interact with the child as if he were still a toddler. They may wish for the attachment they had at an earlier time. A second common mistake, more prevalent among upper-middle-class parents, is pushing the child too fast and punishing him for his mistakes. This is usually done by those parents who want proof that their child is exceptional and don't want to risk anything that might cause the child to be labeled "slow." Always remember, however, that growth is not necessarily a steady process and you may find that your child takes one step forward and two back, or vice versa. (For more information on this subject, you may want to consult the companion book, *When Your Child Grows Up Too Fast.*)

Poor Alec, for example. Because his parents wanted so much for him, they practically deprived him of toddlerhood. When the therapist suggested that Alec have more time to play and experiment, his father was actually relieved. He enjoyed playing with his son, and once all his unrealistic expectations were eliminated, he and Alec spent a lot of time together.

Often, however, if a child takes one step back or regresses, it may be because of other factors. It may be when a new baby is brought into the family or a favorite aunt moves away. Accept and tolerate your child if this happens. The worst thing you can do is to humiliate him or put down his immature behavior.

Remember that a growing child—unless he is suffering from some severe difficulty—will instinctively move toward mastering his world. This is what growth is all about. You can do your part by providing a safe and nurturing environment and by not threatening—or being threatened by—your child's progress. Then growth and development will take care of itself.

STAGE FOUR: THE MIDDLE SCHOOL YEARS (AGES SIX TO TWELVE)

The ages from six to twelve are often called the latent years because they are a relatively quiet time, compared to the years to follow. During this stage, your child will continue to develop his personality and identity, building on his progress up to this time. This is time for alteration and refinement, like putting icing on a cake. And if your child has come up a little short in meeting the challenges of the previous stages, this is also a time when he can catch up.

Most parents experience this as a peaceful time, a time for family outings. Your child probably will enjoy all kinds of activities with you—from camping to watching TV, especially if you allow him to invite a friend.

During the first two to four years of this stage, ages six to ten, your child will begin to move away from his exclusive involvement with the same sex parent and with you generally. This is the time when he will begin to be more active with his peers. By the end of this period, you will seem to be less influential in the child's life and his friends almost too important. This is only temporary, however, and in many ways superficial. Your child still clings to your values, which will help him deal with pressures from his friends.

This is the stage when your child forms his first friendships that last over extended periods of time. In preschool, friendships tended to last only a few days or at the most a few weeks; now your child will begin friendships that last from months to years. This is also a time when children get involved in group play and group activity, and begin to identify with the needs of others. They may even develop for themselves their own preliminary rules for behavior, based on their experiences with other children.

Also during this period, your child will probably adopt an adult of the same sex outside the family as a role model. This could be an aunt, uncle, neighbor, scout leader, teacher, or, even more likely a media personality—movie star, athlete, or even a character in a book, movie, or on TV. The attraction is to a same-sex person who shows confidence, heroism, and initiative—the things that your child probably wants for himself. He will mimic the personality and behavior of this new role model. This will become very important to him and to his own identity. At this stage your child may also be into collecting tangible things that define his self-image—baseball cards or posters, for example.

Many parents become very threatened by these shifting loyalties. They may doubt their child's wisdom, especially in selecting friends. But if you show you're apprehensive and distrustful, your child may take this as your not believing in him or his worth. He may hear your concern as, "If I'm not trusted, perhaps I'm not worthwhile." And as we have seen, such thoughts are destructive to your child's self-esteem.

If the worst scenario happens and your child becomes involved with friends who seem clearly destructive, then professional help may be needed— because generally a healthy child will choose friends who are positive rather than negative. A child who chooses a potentially destructive group of friends probably doesn't feel very good about himself and has a need for self-destructive behavior. It will do you no good, however, to lecture or argue about his friends or put them down. To your child, this would seem like a personal attack. He may think to himself something like, "My parents say I choose the wrong friends, so there must be something wrong with me for liking those people."

It's important to know that sometimes, more usually in the teen years, your child may deliberately choose friends who have different values from you. This is because he is working on completing his identity and is experimenting with his own value system. If you have been helpful and nurturing up to this point, you should feel confident with this experimentation. You should also be aware that this is yet another stage when you might feel that your relationship with your child is not as strong. It is *very* important, however, that you not feel rejected and that you not communicate your negative feelings to your child. The fact is that you are by no means less important. On the contrary, you are even more important at this stage. You are your child's anchor, his foundation, the basic structure to which he is attached by a tight, secure rope. It is the security you offer that actually allows your child to be free to explore. This is true throughout all your child's developmental stages. As he grows, however, it is best if the rope becomes longer and more flexible.

As you might expect, your child's challenge during these years is to be independently productive. In the early school years, his primary task was to take initiative. Now he must learn how to use the initiative successfully. This is the stage when parents most often become concerned with the issue of their child's potential productivity and success in the world. It is not surprising that the skills needed to succeed in these years are more social and intellectual—such as reading and interactions with friends and adults outside of the home. All will have an effect on your child's self-image. If he feels good about himself up to this point, he will trust his ability to have friends. He will trust his teachers, and he will trust himself to complete what he starts.

A child who is hindered at this stage will feel ineffectual and unproductive. He will find social contact is so filled with fear that he will avoid it. If your child is not interested in being with other children or shows hostility toward them, this may be a sign that he needs help.

STAGE FIVE: THE EARLY TEENS

The fifth stage in the development of self-worth and independence is what parents fear the most: adolescence. Even the word sends chills down their spines. While we're primarily concerned here with younger children, all children have to grow up, and it's important for you to realize how your teenager's behavior will be related to his early years.

During adolescence, the child begins the process of evaluating what he has put together. The process is accompanied by great fluctuations in self-esteem. One day the adolescent may be just torn apart by his image of himself and by his interaction with others, and the next day he may feel good. For those children who have progressed more slowly, adolescence may give them the added time they need to complete their personality and sense of self.

It's not unusual that adolescents may find they don't like the prescribed roles available to them. *Jake*, for example, was in the eighth grade and was very interested in being popular. He was not, however, interested in doing things that boys normally do, especially competitive sports. Jake decided that what he really wanted to do was be a cheerleader. He tried out for the squad and became the only boy cheerleader for a junior high school in the city. Jake enjoyed the popularity and didn't mind the few wise-cracks he got from his peers, particularly boys. At the beginning of the next year, when he went out for cheerleader and again made it, one of the girls who lost told him that his classmates were talking behind his back and saying he was "queer." This hurt so much that he quickly resigned from the squad, only to discover the next day that the same girl, who had been first runner-up, took his place. So in three days Jake went from enjoying being a cheerleader, to wanting to quit, and then wanting his old place on the squad back.

At this stage it is your job to avoid teasing your child and not ridicule his behavior or humiliate him for his experiments. (He is engaged in what psychologists call role rehearsal.) Jake's parents, for example, supported his cheerleading and encouraged him the second year. They understood that Jake didn't find the male roles open to him very attractive. So he decided to experiment. Unfortunately, still in the process of developing his identity, he wasn't strong enough to resist negative reaction from his peers.

During the early part of adolescence, children become more interested in relationships outside the family and especially in mixed-sex socializing. Later, a number of romantic relationships will occur, which basically test the adolescent's ability to be more intensely involved with someone outside the family. This is often difficult for parents, because it reduces their control over their child's life. The in-

✴tense attachment to the opposite-sex parent in the early school years and to the same-sex parent in the early middle years finds fulfillment in the friendships and romantic relationships of the teen years. The ability to form loyalties outside of the family and then outside the immediate peer group is important. The social skills and solid sense of identity needed are the same for making connections in the adult world, both personally and professionally. Experimenting with dating helps prepare your child for the later challenge of marrying and having a family.

✴This is why teenagers experiment with going steady. They're testing what it is like to be that involved with one person, to make that person so important. Parents are often concerned that too serious a relationship can take valuable time and effort away from schoolwork. The primary challenge of adolescence, however, is not to learn Shakespeare or mathematics, but to put the finishing touches on the child's personality.

Although your concern for success in school or in extracurricular activities is probably well-meaning, it overlooks the fact that to achieve success at work, a child must know who he is, have good social skills, and be confident. Placing scholastic achievement before everything else is putting the cart before the horse. Emphasizing academics at the expense of personal development almost guarantees failure.

Equally difficult for parents is standing back and seeing a child doing what everybody else is doing. It sometimes seems that self-image and personal identity are achieved at the cost of individuality. During the teenage years, many parents become uncomfortable with their child's need to alter his appearance. You are advised, however, to take only one kind of action if this happens. Encourage such changes. Chances are the child will eventually tire of a new habit or behavior—especially if you can put on a convincing act of being enthusiastic. A sketch presented on TV's "Saturday Night Live" years ago brings home the point.

A teenage son is leaving to go to a classical music concert. Both his parents, wearing matching caftans and smoking a water pipe, are listening to loud rock music. Their son comes in wearing a suit and tie and asks for the keys to the car, and his father says, "Sure, take the big car, the Cadillac." The son hastily replies, "No, no, the VW will do." But his father insists, "No, take the Cadillac, have fun." The son agrees, "OK—but I'll put some gas in it." To which his father replies, "No, don't worry about the gas—go anywhere you want to." And the son says, "Well, I'll be home around eleven." "No, no, no," the father says, "stay out as late as you want to, one or two o'clock— whatever's cool, you know? Your mother and I'll just be here groovin'." And then after the son leaves to pick up his date for the concert, his mother turns to her husband as he takes off his caftan, and says, "Dear, how long do you think we have to keep this up?" And he says to her, "I don't know, but it seems to be working."

You should not make issues out of trivial matters of dress and hairstyles. There are enough important things to worry about. Just as your toddler needs to explore his physical environment, your teenager needs to explore his culture.

During this discussion of the various developmental stages that occur within your child's life, we have suggested a few principles you may use to help your child ease through childhood with maximum success and minimum problems. The next part of this book offers more specific suggestions to help in the growth and development of your child's self-image.

Part III
How to Help

The majority of the suggestions we offer here are preventive and assume that your child is not currently suffering from any significant developmental "lags" in growing up. If after reading Part Two you feel your child has problems and you have been unable to help by being encouraging and supportive and providing a safe harbor in your family, you should perhaps seek professional help. If you are unsure of how to do so, you will find helpful guidelines at the end of this section.

HELPFUL HINT #1—PROVIDE CONSISTENT, LOVING CARE DURING INFANCY

If there is any time when family stability is essential,

it is in these first years of your infant's life. Your baby's need for continuity of care must be given priority. It is absolutely crucial during this period from birth to approximately two years old that an infant learn he can trust his environment.

If you find it necessary to hire someone to be the primary caretaker, or even someone to share the role part-time, it's important that this be someone who is able and willing to meet the baby's needs. In looking for a caretaker, you should seek someone who is intelligent, dedicated, and stable. Professional nannies are usually the best choice, but they may be hard to find and expensive. College students, especially those who are majoring in some aspect of child development, can be less expensive. Rotating babysitters, however, is inadvisable, even if it's only for a few months.

It is also important that you watch your infant to see whether he seems happy and responsive and enjoys lots of stimulation. He should enjoy being touched and respond to your physical expressions of emotion. Other healthy behavior to watch for includes reaching for objects and people and a general response to his environment.

If your child is well physically, eats well and, except for temporary bouts of illness, appears healthy and happy and enjoys stimulation, then he is learning to trust, and he'll be a happy and healthy toddler.

Having a baby is an important event. You should plan for it. Your infant needs quality *and* quantity of attention, as well as consistent care. If caretaking is well provided in these formative years, as your child grows, you can rotate with each other and with a nanny in caretaking. Later, the amount of time you spend with your child will not be as important. (For additional views on early parenting, you may wish to consult *How to Be a Good Role Model for Your Child.*)

HELPFUL HINT #2—SET LIMITS THAT HELP YOUR TODDLER EXPLORE AND DISCOVER THINGS

In the early years, from infancy through toddlerhood and into the early school years, it is important for you to provide a safe environment. You'll want to provide maximum safety while still allowing your child to be free to explore spontaneously.

Apply the following guidelines to create a safe environment:

1. Provide toys that are both safe and suitable to your child's age.

2. Investigate neighborhood play equipment in public parks and playgrounds; teach your child to play only where it's safe. If you live in an apartment or condominium complex, get involved in decision making about your child's play areas.

3. Check your own interests. Are you being selfless with your children and being angry about it? Your needs and your child's don't have to conflict.

Maybe you'll feel comfortable establishing some private time for yourself. If you've planned to take a bubble bath to relax and just as you step into the tub, your child wants your attention, there's nothing wrong with saying, "Mommy is going to take a bath right now. After that, I'll be out to play with you." Usually children want to see their parents happy. It is often parents who fail to make such demands on their children. If you're providing your child with the love and care he requires, he will be willing to give you what you need also.

4. Your home needs to be made "childproof." For your child to be happy, productive, independent, and creative, childproofing the house is a must. Most parents are sensitive to the dangers that may threaten children, such as access to medicines, or toxic chemicals, tools, or kitchen implements. You should also take pains to remove any valuables from your child's play area. If you have special possessions, be sure to put them out of reach of children, perhaps in an "adult" room that is off-limits. In this way, you protect your own possessions and eliminate the constant need to watch your child or complain if he damages your property.

5. Don't require behavior beyond your child's capabilities. If you plan dinner out as a family, go to a restaurant where children are expected and other people will tolerate a certain amount of childhood's unruliness. Or leave your child at home with a sitter. Dinner out is not something your toddler will particularly like anyhow.

HELPFUL HINT #3—HELP YOUR CHILD BE CREATIVE

During the early school years, you should help your child learn to take initiative. The best way is to bring out his creativity. Special occasions and holidays provide excellent opportunities for creative activities that you may not have time for on a day-to-day basis. Instead of buying a Halloween costume, for example, provide an old sheet or piece of scrap material and help your child make a costume for himself.

If your child has difficulty deciding what to make and says, "Oh, Daddy, I can't do this," don't step in and solve the problem. *Jackson*, a five-year-old tomboy, for example, was stumped about what to wear to her preschool's Halloween party. Her conversation with her father went as follows:

Jackson: *Daddy, I don't have a costume to wear to the Halloween party next month. Can we go down to the store to buy one?*

Dad: *Well, we could do that, but don't you think it might be more fun to make something yourself? Then you can be just exactly what you want to be.*

Jackson: *Yeah, but I don't know what I want to be.*

Dad: *Well, what do you like to play?*

Jackson: *I like playing with my robot gun.*

Dad: *Well, how about being a space explorer?*

Jackson: *No, Richard is going to do that.*
Dad: *Anything else?*
Jackson: *I like playing with my Ninja sword that Mom bought me in Hawaii.*
Dad: *Let's think about what a Ninja looks like. I'll get the encyclopedia.*
Jackson: *OK, but I know Ninjas wear headbands and baggy pants. I could wear a pair of old pajamas if Mom will let me and make a headband and. . . .*

Because Jackson's father wanted his child to have a chance to see what fun it would be to make something herself, he was patient. But he was also prepared to help her when she came up with a suggestion of her own.

Christmas and Hanukkah obviously provide great opportunity for your entire family to make things together. Instead of buying gifts, you could make it a family rule that everybody must give at least one homemade present to everyone else in the family. This is a chance for four- and five-year-olds to work together with the family in a creative project. Above all, do not be critical of what your child comes up with. Always be encouraging and enthusiastic. Use careful words of encouragement about how he might do better the next time.

A child who doesn't start things on his own, who generally resists being creative and spontaneous, and who is not excited about things he can do, needs help. If additional attention from you proves to be insufficient, don't hesitate to seek family counseling.

If your child constantly asks, "What can I do now?" or complains, "I'm bored," he needs lots of your attention. There are several things you can do to help your child be independent.

1. Listen to your child and try to find out why he is nervous or apprehensive about what he's supposed to do.
2. Be understanding and don't be critical. Be caring and interested.
3. Gently encourage your child when he tries things on his own.
4. Provide opportunities to try independent projects.

✳ Encouragement and enthusiasm of any small steps your child takes in starting his own projects will go a long way. Creativity in arts and crafts shows that your child has the ability to be creative in other areas. A child who builds caves in the living room is much more likely to want a microscope or a toy car he can disassemble than a child who spends his time watching television. Be aware, however, that at this age, children are not always able to tell the difference between size, weight, and volume. So if your have a burgeoning scientists in your garage, be sure that you are on hand to help put the chemicals together. Better yet, encourage a child with a scientific bent to spend his energy collecting and classifying things— bugs and plants, for example. Children at this age get a great deal of satisfaction out of classifying and labeling things.

HELPFUL HINT #4—BE SENSITIVE TO YOUR TEENAGER'S NEEDS

In the teenage years, parents tend to overreact to the various types of peer group fads their children want to participate in. They fear perhaps that their children will be harmed in the long run. It is advisable, however, for you to evaluate which things are truly harmful and which are only small experiments in rebellion typical of the teenage years. For example, one young teenager, *Maxime*, had a long-running debate with her mother about the color of her hair. Most of Maxime's friends had taken to dying a contrasting streak in the front of their hairstyle. Maxime had told her mother that she was going to do the same thing, and her mother forbade her to do so. When Maxime asked why, her mother admitted to the fear that the dyed streak would give people the wrong impression of Maxime and that it certainly wasn't a good thing if she was going to be looking for a job during the summer.

Actually Maxime's mother should have been happy that the dyed hair was all that her child was interested in. She should have accepted this small rebellion and actually encouraged it. For Maxime, dying a streak in her hair was not an overtly destructive act nor would it affect anyone else—except perhaps her mother's sensibilities. Instead of understanding, Maxime's mother chose to express her irrational fears that Maxime would wear this dyed streak for the rest of her life or that the dyed hair was the first step toward falling in with the wrong crowd. By her actions, Maxime's mother was demonstrating a typical mistake. She was attacking the wrong issue, endangering her child's trust in her and increasing the possibility that her daughter would do something that really would be bad for her own well-being.

HELPFUL HINT #5—SAY WHAT YOU MEAN, AND MEAN WHAT YOU SAY

As we said before, happy families share good ways of communicating. Parents often complain that their children don't communicate. Although often this may seem to be true, the problem lies in *how* family members choose to communicate. Communication is an ongoing process and is always present in one form or another in any family. The important thing is the type of communication the family uses.

In her work on family interaction, Virginia Satir has identified two general familial communication patterns. She describes them as double-level message and single-level message patterns. Double-level messages mean that a person's words say one thing and his body language says something else. In most situations, the real message is expressed in the person's facial expressions, body positions, muscle tones, breathing tempo, and voice quality.

For healthy and efficient family interaction, it's best if what you say and how you act mean the same thing. Unfortunately, too often this is not the case.

The younger your child, the more attuned he will be to what you do. The messages a baby responds to, for example, are overwhelmingly from physical contact—holding and touching by parents or caretakers—as well as from the infant's attempt to reach out and touch things in his world. The senses are the infant's primary means of communicating. As a child grows older, he becomes experienced in speaking as well as feeling. The truth is, however, that body language is the most telling form of communication for most human beings—children and adults alike.

In unhappy families communication is indirect and confusing. Satir has described four double-message patterns that often exist in such families, usually because one person establishes a pattern that the rest of the family follows. That person might be a *placator*. The placator agrees to whatever is said, while his actions say he is helpless and has no other choice. What the placator is really saying is, "I will agree with whatever you say, because I feel I have no power in this situation." In order to feel good about himself, the placator needs other people to feel that he's OK. It is a fearful pattern for the person and for other family members, because the placator often *seems* to agree with what is being said even though he really doesn't. He is likely to quietly go off and do his own thing, even though in conversation he has actually agreed to do something completely different.

In families with a placator, there is almost always his opposite, the *blamer*. In conversation the blamer is almost always antagonistic and judgmental—it is a communication strategy for which the placator makes an excellent foil. With the blamer body language is especially revealing. It reinforces his message but doesn't say much about what is really going on inside him. As he is expressing his opinions verbally, his body is likely to indicate that he considers himself to be in charge of the situation. He may move threateningly toward the person to whom he's speaking or deliberately turn his back to close off someone else from the conversation. Emotionally, however, the blamer feels lonely and unsuccessful at making contact with other family members. His bluster is a cover for feelings of isolation and insecurity.

A third communication style found in families is what Satir calls the *computer*. This is a person who is reasonable to a fault, who uses language a president of a company might use with a board of directors. A typical computer statement might be formalized to the point that it's silly and has little to do with what the conversation is really about. An example would be a father who is upset by the condition of his son's room but can only express it in roundabout terms, saying, "If one were to observe carefully, one might notice the amount of dirt that has accumulated in this particular bedroom." A computer usually uses subtle sarcasm, which the family may try to excuse as being humorous, intellectual, or satirical. Although the computer's body language appears to be cool and is designed to keep people at a distance, in fact such a person feels vulnerable inside. He depends on his ability to intellectualize his feelings as his link to the rest of the family.

Finally, there is the *distractor*, who deliberately stays tuned out of the conversation, especially if it's about an important family issue. The family may be discussing a place to have dinner, and the distractor will suddenly interrupt with a story from the evening news. Like the computer, the distractor's body implies that he is removed from the conversation; for example, eye contact with the other family members will be minimal or nonexistent. Emotionally the distractor is saying to himself, "I don't really belong here. I don't have a place in this situation," but instead of actively withdrawing, he attempts to interrupt the positive flow of communication among family members.

↙ The opposite of these destructive double-edged communication styles is the healthier *single-level* communication pattern, in which what each person says verbally corresponds to his body language and to what he is really feeling. This Satir calls *leveling*.

Relationships within families that adopt this single-level pattern tend to be honest and open. Because all family members are aware not only of family standards but also of the goals and agenda of the family—as individuals and as a group—the need to guess what is going on is diminished. Parents and children alike know where they stand, and this leads to positive feelings of security, competence, and self-esteem. Using "I" statements is an important element in leveling conversation. When family members are angry about something, they express that anger directly and don't feel bad about it.

Without such open and straightforward communication patterns, it's virtually impossible for you to inform your child of what you expect of him, what the rules for his behavior are, or what he's done wrong if he makes a mistake. Even worse, it's next to impossible for your child to tell you what is happening with him. The guessing and manipulation that goes on when communication is not direct and honest is always threatening to a child's self-esteem and minimizes chances that you can provide the warm, nurturing environment your child needs for healthy development.

You should strive to make what you say and what you do coincide so that the messages you communicate to your child are clear and concise and require little interpretation. Through the first years of his life, you are your child's role model. If you demonstrate a clear, single-message level of communication, he will learn that this is the best way, and he will be much better for your efforts.

HELPFUL HINT #6—SHOW HOW TO EXPRESS EMOTION

As individuals we seek others' understanding. Being known and understood by others in our world protects us from feeling lonely. Despite this universal desire to express ourselves and be appreciated, we often don't listen with understanding, especially when expressing emotions. It is important, however, from the very first interactions you have with your child, that you express your feelings and emotions in the same way you want your children to do so. Here are some ways of doing this:

● Tell your child your feelings without blaming or accusing your child of causing the negative feelings you are expressing. It is much better to say, for example, "When you run around this room yelling, I get angry and upset because I can't hear on the telephone." You should *not* say, "You are a bad boy when you run around screaming while I'm on the phone." The first is an honest expression of emotion and provides a good model; the second blames the child and will likely turn him off.

● Separate the child from his behavior. To label a child with such expressions as, "You are bad," or "You are good," rather than, "I like what you do," or "I don't like what you are doing," can be confusing and make him feel bad.

● In young children, encourage physical expression of anger. In preschool and even in the early elementary years, your child will probably have a very difficult time following your model and putting his feelings in words. He will want to express his emotions physically. He may jump up and down when he's happy or stomp his feet and hit things when he's angry. You can help encourage emotional expression by providing things that make it easier for him. Paints, crayons, punching bags, pillows, and stuffed animals are good to have available, and using them helps the child work out his feelings without being destructive.

You should also be aware that anger is a normal emotion, but it can sometimes be used by your child to cover some other emotion he can't express. Listening carefully to how your child expresses anger can sometimes give you an idea of what is really going on. Maybe he's frustrated by something that happened in school, or hurt because he had an argument with a friend. Anger is a very primitive emotion. Because it's close to the surface, it's easy for children to express. The idea is to help your child uncover the real cause of his feelings so he can feel comfortable expressing them appropriately.

● Recognize the reason for temper tantrums. When your child becomes locked in the grip of a temper tantrum, it's usually for one of two reasons. He may feel out of control and be expressing it physically, or he may be attempting to control you or someone else in your family. A child learns quickly how to get his way; thus if you give in to him to stop the temper tantrum, you'll just encourage him and you'll never find out what was causing him to be so angry. Try to physically restrain the child, hold him, tell him you love him and care. Once he's calmed down, you can try to figure out what's wrong. If your daughter is running around the house out of control, try soothing her with words like, "I know you are really upset and I can really understand how you feel." If she responds by saying, "Let me go!" say, "I am going to let you go. But right now I want to help you."

● Eventually you will want to establish times and places for expressing emotion. As your child becomes more comfortable expressing his feelings with other family members, you'll want to start teaching when and where it's okay to let you know what he's feeling. This will likely vary with your child's age and development. It's probably better for a small child to express his emotions immediately. If you are out shopping, for example, and your child becomes angry or frustrated about something, you can take him to the car and try to resolve the problem if it can't wait. With an older child, you will be more successful explaining that you want to wait until you get home to discuss what's bothering him. There is nothing wrong with families having rules about expressing emotions in public places. Many emotions are better expressed in the privacy of the family, especially if the whole family is involved with the problem the child is upset about. As a child grows, one of his challenges will be to learn self-restraint. Your message should always be: 1) it's okay to be emotional and express it; 2) it's better to find out why you're upset so you can learn from it; and 3) we all have to use common sense. A young child running around a supermarket screaming is not doing anyone any good, especially if he does it mainly to get your attention. (Ignore these outbursts and be sure to praise and encourage him when he does good things.)

• Don't try to protect your child. Remember, your child's exploration of his world involves experiencing emotional reactions—and communicating them to other people. Emotional experience is vital to life. Our technological society often seems to stifle emotion, perhaps because of the fear that it keeps people from being productive. Only unexpressed or misunderstood emotion is a problem. Be aware that unexpressed feelings of anger can lead to depression. In families where anger is hidden, both parents and children are likely to be withdrawn and depressed, with a low sense of self-worth. Always model to your children that feelings—good or bad—are OK.

There are several benefits to expressing emotions. First, there is simple relief. Our bodies tend to relax after we have expressed our emotions, especially when the emotions have been accepted by others. Negative feelings such as anger, sadness, and fear lose their destructive power. The quickest way to rid ourselves of a negative emotion is actually to encourage its expression. Furthermore, the actual expression of emotion may help you and your child clarify the underlying cause of his feelings, which may help him to avoid similar situations in the future. He'll know to walk away from the bully the next time he taunts him, for example, or not to try to play ball with the big boys until he's a better player. Most important, releasing emotion frees us from its grasp so we can get on with more pleasant things.

HELPFUL HINT #7—LISTEN ACTIVELY

Your child's intellectual ability is related to his emotional health. Children who suffer from what we commonly call "pent-up" emotions don't do as well in their schoolwork, especially if it involves sustained interest and attention. The energy necessary for intellectual productivity and creative activity simply is unavailable. Such a child is likely to withdraw and be alienated from the rest of the family. If you question him, he won't be able to explain his discomfort. When your child's behavior differs significantly from his expressed feelings, something is definitely amiss, and your child probably doesn't know what it is or how to explain it to you.

What can you do with a child who constantly sulks and whines but denies that anything is the matter? In such a situation, a successful strategy is what Thomas Gordon calls "active listening." First you must set aside time to speak to your child without distractions. Then you must be able to draw out his feelings and emotions without being judgmental or too quick to offer a solution.

The following is a brief description of the active listening technique:

● *Use "door openers."*—These are responses that invite your child to share his ideas and feelings but don't communicate any judgment about his feelings of discomfort. Common door openers you can use to respond to what your child says include, "Oh, that's interesting; tell me more," or, "I see what you mean," or, "Boy, that must really be important to you." The invitation to speak encourages your child to start and—you hope—continue sharing what is bothering him.

● *Listen, don't talk.*—Most parents are upset by their child's distress, and, in an effort to help him overcome his pain, they often find themselves doing all the talking. Remember, you want to explore your child's feelings, so don't force the conversation to go in a specific, predetermined direction. This will require patience because a young child particularly doesn't organize his thoughts in the same way that adults do. Especially when upset, a child will find it very difficult to articulate his feelings.

● *Listen for meaning, not just words or information.* Respond to the meaning of the child's message and restrain your impulses to offer evaluation,
advice, or analysis. And when you respond, be careful
not to use the child's own words, but instead indicate
that you understand what he is saying by repeating it
in your own words.

● *Be attuned to both verbal and nonverbal
expression.*—Keeping in mind that your child wants
to be understood from his own point of view when
he expresses his emotions, you need to "listen" to
both verbal and nonverbal messages so that your
child feels he has really been understood. This requires paying a great deal of attention to the meanings behind what he's saying and then repeating it
back to him, again in your own words..

● *Allow your child to develop his own solutions.*—Always remember that your goal is to offer
feedback your child can use to solve his problem.
Your goal is for your child to get in touch with his
feelings and understand the relationship between his
feelings and the problem. You don't want to solve his
problems for him. Listening to anyone—adult or
child—express emotions is not the time for logic.
Problem-solving necessarily takes a back seat at the
moment emotions are being expressed.

● *Don't push.*—No matter how far you attempt to open the door, your child may not be prepared to discuss whatever is bothering him. Respect
that he may not be ready to open up at that particular
time. Also, never extend that open-door invitation
unless you are sure that *you* have time and attention
to actively listen to your child. There is nothing
worse for a child than to fear that he can't trust his

parents. If you succeed in getting your child to express his feelings and then abruptly terminate the conversation because of other demands on your time, you are doing both of you a great disservice.

• *Avoid trying to find out why* your child is experiencing particular emotions intensely. It is more beneficial to his sense of self-esteem in the long run to allow the expression of the emotion. If you help him by listening, then repeating what he said, then the child may begin to figure out what made him so upset in the first place. This is especially true of older children, who are capable of understanding the "why" of their feelings.

• *Always remember to put yourself in your child's place.* Expressing emotion is a risky business for parents and children alike. As adults we appreciate an understanding and nonjudgmental ear when we're upset or frustrated. Your child needs even more empathy and loving listening when he's attempting to express how he feels. He will need to trust that you care and that he's safe with you.

To demonstrate how active listening works, let's take the example of *Sherri*, age seven, who has come home from school in a black mood. She walks into the kitchen where her mother is busy fixing dinner and slams her books down on the kitchen table. It's an action that Sherri's mother can hardly be expected *not* to notice and, as such, seems to call for some reaction. Her mother decides that this is a time for active listening.

Mom: *What's the matter, Sherri? Did something happen at school today?*

Sherri: *Yeah.*

Mom: *Well, if you want, I'd like to hear about it, but can you wait until I finish putting the roast in the oven for dinner? Why don't you get yourself a glass of milk and a piece of cake?*

Sherri: *[sulking] OK.*

Mom: *[after putting the roast in the oven] OK, now I'm all yours. Tell me what you're upset about.*

Sherri: *I hate school.*

Mom: *I didn't know that. I thought you were having a good time. Did something bad happen today?*

Sherri: *Yes, it did.*

Mom: *Do you want to tell me about it?*

Sherri: *[obviously frustrated] My teacher hates me, and I hate her!*

Mom: *I see. Do you want to tell me what happened? Only if you want to.*

Sherri: *She told me I was being bad in class.*

Mom: *And you think that's not fair?*

Sherri: *Yes, because Robbie was talking to me, and all I did was answer back.*

Mom: *Well, if you didn't do anything, you must feel pretty bad.*

Sherri: *Yes, Mom, I do because Robbie was bothering me all morning long, and it was only when I tried to tell him to be quiet that my teacher noticed us talking.*

Mom: *That must have been very frustrating for you when you were just trying to do something right.*

Sherri: *It was, and I don't know what to do about it.*

This hypothetical conversation continued, and Sherri and her mom together developed a way for Sherri to speak to her teacher and tell her how she felt about what happened. Since this was the first time that Sherri's mom had heard about a problem between her daughter and her teacher, she decided not to intervene unless the problem continued. Sherri's mother listened to her daughter and understood why she was bothered, but offered solutions to the *cause* of her feelings *only after Sherri told her how she felt.* Sherri at first wanted her mom to speak to the teacher but her mom knew that it would be best for her child to talk to her teacher herself.

And so it is that active listening requires that you accept the fact that basically your child will need to learn to solve some of his own problems, that you can't protect him from a bully, for example, or rush to school everytime there's a problem with the teacher. Offer concern, care, and help, but refrain from initiating a solution itself, unless it is something that is drastically beyond your child's influence and control.

HELPFUL HINT #8—USE CONSTRUCTIVE DISCIPLINE

There are essentially two ways families discipline their children. Although the two are diametrically opposed to each other, both are equally negative. The authoritarian style, in which parents assume they know what is best for their children and exert rigid and unbending control over them leads to fear and repression and inhibits a child's growth. Overpermissiveness, on the other hand, leaves children in a perpetual state of limbo, never knowing what the standards are for behavior or when they've met them. In authoritarian families there is little room for choice; in permissive families the opportunity for choice is so great that it is debilitating. The power is in the hands of the children who actually fear it.

Authoritative parenting fails because parents really don't have an all-pervasive power over their children. Additionally, children faced with such a rigid system will ultimately rebel—either aggressively or by passive withdrawal. Compliance motivated by fear of either physical or emotional punishment is false.

Fortunately for parents and children alike, there is an alternative. It's called democratic parenting. Rudolph Driekurs, one of its most articulate proponents, feels that children naturally want to do what is right. This means that a child who is misbehaving is actually discouraged and upset. What you need in such situations is to be encouraging and positive. Driekurs's recommendations are actually a variation of the age-old practical wisdom of cause and effect. The basic strategy is simple—allow your child to understand and, if necessary, suffer the consequences of his actions.

As Driekurs points out, there are some occasions where consequence of action is *natural*, as when we forget to go to the store before it closes and suffer with no dinner, or when a child neglects to toss dirty clothes in the laundry basket and has no clean clothes for school the next day. *Logical* consequences require that you take action, or intervene. Your second-grader, for example, forgets her lunch for the third day in a row and calls you—as she has the previous two days—to ask you to bring the lunch to school. You remind her that it is the third time she has forgotten her lunch and that you have an appointment and don't have the time to bring it to her. It is not likely to take long for her to understand that the consequence of forgetting her lunch is going hungry.

Ronald and his jackets provide another excellent example of using cause and effect as a constructive disciplinary technique. Ronald is a twelve-year-old who during a particularly difficult six months couldn't remember what he did with his jacket. He would stay overnight at a friend's house and leave his jacket, only to find out that someone else had taken it. Or he would leave a jacket on the school bus. His parents tried different means of punishing him, from grounding Ronald to cutting out his allowance. Nothing worked until Ronald's father hatched the idea of showing Ronald the consequences of his action. The third time Ronald came home with his jacket missing, his father announced that on Saturday they were making a trip to the bank. "What for?" asked Ronald. "So you can take out money from your savings account to buy another jacket," said his father. Which is what Ronald and his father did. As the two withdrew the money and went to buy the child his third jacket in less than a month, his father told him, "Now, Ronald, this is the last jacket we're going to buy for you.

You've spent your own money on this one, and if you lose it, you won't get another." The message was clear. Ronald was able to hold on to his jacket for the rest of the winter.

Although at first it might be a bit difficult to think of your son going without a jacket or your daughter without her lunch, it is important to remember that these are only temporary situations which your child is capable of remedying. If he does so, he will be better off because a knowledge of cause and effect is crucial to your child for life. Your child needs to see the logical results of his actions. He needs to move forward in a positive way instead of feeling bad about something he did or did not do in the past.

HELPFUL HINT #9—USE DEMOCRATIC DECISION MAKING

All organizations must make decisions to accomplish goals and to enhance the well-being of members. Families are no exception. Establishing guidelines for expressing feelings and for behavior generally is an important part of the process involved in what is called democratic decision making. Democratic decision making and rule setting are based on the principle that a decision must have the willing support of the group members to be effective. Obviously this complements the technique of democratic discipline. The premise is that each person in the family, regardless of age or circumstances, has a right to the pursuit of individual happiness and respect as a separate person.

Communication is essential to the democratic process. You must encourage open and honest communication without double-edged meanings. You must provide your child with opportunities to make his opinions and needs known, and you must allow your child to be responsible for abiding by the decisions the family makes. Obviously, very young children are unable to actively participate in this process, but you should at least model the behavior so that as your child grows older, this will come naturally.

Let's take the case of thirteen-year-old *Bruce*, who agreed to clean the garage once a week in exchange for an extra fifty cents in his allowance. This particular week, Bruce has put the job off until the only time to do it is Saturday afternoon. Bruce is faced with a dilemma; he has also been invited to spend Saturday afternoon at the beach with his friends. He goes to his mother and says to her, "Mom, I don't want to clean the garage, I want to go to the beach." To which his mother should reply, "But you made a commitment and the painter is coming tomorrow to paint the garage floor. If you don't clean it, then I'll have to. We agreed that you would do this, and you really should have thought about this at the beginning of the week, not now." Bruce will probably be angry that he will miss going to the beach with his friends, and it would be best for his mother to acknowledge his anger at the same time she reminds him of his commitment. "You're really angry that you've agreed to clean the garage and now this opportunity to go with your friends to the beach has come up. I know that feels very bad. I know that you are angry and upset. But you did agree to do it, and I therefore think you should clean the garage."

Another essential element of democratic decision making is understanding that each person's actions affect the lives of others. It is a lesson we all have to learn in life—the sooner the better. A child who feels that he is taken into consideration when rules or decisions are made will see how his desires will affect the rest of the family. He will understand that what he wants must take into consideration the rest of the family and understand that he can't always have things exactly the way he wants.

SEEKING PROFESSIONAL HELP

Traditional social supports for the family don't exist in today's world of two-income households, single-parent families, and mobile careers. Thus it should come as no surprise that families often find that they need help. If this is the case with your family, you should not feel bad. In fact, an annual visit to a family therapist who knows your family members and the issues your family is facing can be as important as your yearly checkup with the family doctor.

Unfortunately, families who think nothing of calling a plumber or an electrician to fix a routine problem often wince at the thought of seeking counseling for a troubled child or to help solve a family crisis. They blame the troubled child as the cause of their problems and are angry at him. If you can approach therapy as a constructive rather than a destructive process, all family members will benefit, problems will be solved much more quickly, and everyone will be able to get on with their lives.

When does a child need professional therapy? The answer is complex, but a good rule of thumb is if, at any given developmental stage, you see that your child is living life more on the downside, therapy may be well advised. If a nurturing environment with sympathetic, active listening doesn't help, then a therapist can probably provide advice and counsel. As a general rule it is wise to allow several weeks to two or three months to work out the difficulties within the family, particularly if your child is less than six years old. If things don't flow smoothly after a while, then find someone who can help. The older the child, the longer it may take to turn behavior around, which means that it is best to correct such problems in early childhood.

If you do seek help while the child is in these early years, it is likely that you will be involved in the process.

Sometimes parents are uncomfortable with the thought of being "patients." You should know, however, that modern family counselors regard the family as a total unit, where what each person does affects the others. Your best bet, then, is to choose someone who is used to working with families, who understands family relationships and can involve everyone in the counseling process. (Generally speaking, psychiatrists and psychologists don't always think in terms of relationships and families; their focus is more directly on the individual, although many are experienced in family therapy.)

As with all of the other suggestions we've offered

here, we urge you to stop a moment and think about what's really going on in your family. Then, if necessary, consider taking advantage of professional help. Why fool around with something as important as your child's sense of worth and well-being? It's his key to taking an active place in the world and projecting to others an image of the inner glow he feels inside himself.

For more advice on deciding on a therapist and what you can expect, check with the companion books, *When Your Child Grows Up Too Fast* and *How To Be a Good Role Model for Your Child.*

CONCLUSION

Although much of what we have said here may seem obvious, many parents nonetheless have great trouble in helping their children through the essential childhood tasks that lead to building a positive sense of self and a solid identity. The information presented here provides a framework for you to help your child feel good about himself and his potential. Parenting requires a great deal of effort; why not put it in the right place?

Although the family has experienced drastic changes within this century, it nonetheless remains our best hope for raising strong, able, secure children. You have the wherewithal to make the time your child spends with you—from infancy through adolescence—very productive, meaningful, and joyous years. We hope you will find this book an aid in doing just that.

REFERENCES

To learn more about how family systems and communication processes affect self-esteem, we suggest these two very readable and enjoyable books:

Briggs, Dorothy. *Your Child's Self-Esteem.* New York: Doubleday, 1970.

Satir, V. *Peoplemaking.* Palo Alto: Science and Behavior Books, 1972.

For specific techniques for effective parenting, especially on active listening and disciplining children, we suggest these two widely used books:

Dreikurs, R. *Children, the Challenge.* New York: E. P. Dutton, 1987.

Gordon, Thomas. *PET: Parent Effectiveness Training.* New York: The New American Library, 1975.

For more about interpersonal communication processes in general and the way in which they affect the quality of nearly every aspect of your life, consult these two books:

James, M. and D. Jongeward. *Born to Win*. Reading, Mass.: Addison-Wesley, 1971.

Miller, S. E. Nunnally, and D. Wackmen. *Alive and Aware: How to Improve Your Relationships Through Better Communication*. Minneapolis, Minn.: Interpersonal Communication Programs, 1975.

For more about human development from birth to death, we suggest this very comprehensive and readable text on the subject:

Newman, Barbara, M., and Philip R. Newman. *Development Through Life: A Psychosocial Approach*, Fourth Edition. Chicago: The Dorsey Press, 1987.

ADDITIONAL REFERENCES FOR THE ADOLESCENT YEARS

Blos, P. *On Adolescence.* New York: Free Press, 1962.

Erikson, Erik. *Childhood and Society.* New York: W. W. Norton, 1963.

Erikson, Erik. *Identity, Youth and Crisis.* New York: W. W. Norton, 1968.

Guidana, Vittorio, F. *Complexity of the Self: A Developmental Approach to Psychopathology and Therapy.* New York: The Guilford Press, 1987.

Lefrancois, Guy R. *Adolescents.* Belmont, Calif.: Wadsworth, 1981.

Mishne, Judith M. *Clinical Work with Adolescents.* New York: Macmillan, 1987.

Piaget, Jean. *Psychology of Intelligence.* Totowa, N.J.: Littlefield, Adams and Co., 1966.

Schaefer, Charles E., James M. Briesmeister, and Maureen Fitton. *Family Therapy Techniques for*

Problem Behaviors of Children and Teenagers.
San Francisco: Jossey-Bass Inc., 1984.

Please note: If you've decided to visit a family counselor but don't know how to find one, the national
office of the American Association of Marriage and
Family Therapy will be glad to provide phone num-
bers of therapists in your area. Their number is
(202) 429-1825.